THE NOVELLO BOC

BRITIS
FOLKSONGS

For mixed-voice choirs

With an introduction by Jeremy Summerly

THE NOVELLO BOOK *of*
BRITISH FOLKSONGS

For mixed-voice choirs

With an introduction by Jeremy Summerly

NOVELLO

Published by
Novello Publishing Limited
14-15 Berners Street,
London W1T 3LJ, UK.

Exclusive Distributors:
Music Sales Limited
Distribution Centre, Newmarket Road,
Bury St Edmunds, Suffolk IP33 3YB, UK.

Music Sales Pty Limited
Level 4, 30-32 Carrington Street,
Sydney, NSW 2000 Australia.

Order No. NOV164450
ISBN 978-1-78305-416-9

Music processed by Paul Ewers Music Design.
Project Manager and Editor: Jonathan Wikeley.

Printed in the EU.

www.musicsalesclassical.com

Contents

Introduction

The word 'folk' was used by Chaucer. Yet it wasn't until the early-19th century that the term 'folklore' was coined in English, and it wasn't until several decades thereafter that the term 'folksong' was devised. But although the folksong label was a late-19th century one, the genre had existed for centuries. Nowadays, folk can be as unhelpful a musical label as classical, pop, or jazz. To be sure, listeners and performers of Western music broadly know what those descriptors mean. But there are many works that are impossible to classify under a single heading. The essence, for instance, of Stravinsky's primitivistic ballet *The Rite of Spring* – these days a mainstay of the modern classical canon – is Lithuanian folk melody; in 1973 the electric folk group Steeleye Span marketed the renaissance-harmonised medieval hymn 'Gaudete' as a folk-rock carol, with an enviable degree of commercial success; and certain well-known 'folk' songs are actually 19th-century music-hall songs, whose self-parodies were so expertly composed that their performances now perennially elicit tears rather than jeers. Purists may wince at the contents of the present volume, since many of its songs are only peripherally 'folk'. And even the genuine folk songs (whatever that really means) are served up here in choral arrangements that would surely be frowned upon in Ballyshannon or Cambridge in early August.

Analysis of musical repertories that have been transmitted by oral tradition reveals that words are modified in the re-telling more readily than pitches – embellishment and alteration of both words and music are an inevitable part of the process. And while a glossary of the words of folk songs would be large, the building blocks of domestic modal melody are few. In other words, the vocabulary of folk song is rich – albeit frequently stylised – while folk melody is a simple (though subtle) affair, whose modes rely on carefully formulaic variation of timbre, articulation, and texture *in performance* in order to transmit the real value of the genre. Sometimes words are simplified through apparent lack of care and absence of sophistication, yet at other times that simplification occurs for sensitive and laudable reasons, for instance to make popular material suitable for the mouths and ears of children. And sometimes melodies (whether vocal or instrumental) evolve a stepwise pattern that all but obscures the tune's original shape. Printed versions are also a mixed blessing: on the one hand they carve in stone sanitised versions of words and music; yet they also help to preserve the songs for posterity.

The 19th-century folk revival owed much to the pioneering Anglican priests John Broadwood (1798-1864) and Sabine Baring-Gould (1834-1924). Figures like Frank Kidson (1855-1926) and Lucy Broadwood (1858-1929) – niece of John Broadwood – helped to found the Folk-Song Society in 1898 (the Welsh chapter was inaugurated eight years later). The Irish composer Charles Stanford (1852-1924) served on the first committee of the Folk-Song Society, and in 1901 Cecil Sharp (1859-1924) joined the group. In the two decades stretching from 1903 to 1923, Sharp came to be regarded as the early-20th century's finest collector and disseminator of English folk song. It was homesickness during Sharp's ten-year sojourn in Adelaide and the unwelcome dominance of German musical thinking in England at the opening of the 20th century that made Sharp such a passionate advocate for English folk culture. In the event, Sharp collected well over 3,000 English tunes (beginning in Somerset) and some in America as well.

Alongside his contribution to the secular revival of folk song, Ralph Vaughan Williams (1872-1958) made his presence felt as musical editor of the *English Hymnal*, published in 1906. Folk songs from around Europe and America were pressed into service as hymn tunes as a result of Vaughan Williams's open-eared genius. It is ironic that the successful musical editorship of the *English Hymnal* is one of the achievements for which Vaughan Williams is fondly remembered, because he initially turned the project down. Vaughan Williams only capitulated when the creator of the *English Hymnal*, Rev. Percy Dearmer (1867-1936), remarked that in the event of Vaughan Williams's refusal to participate, Dearmer would be forced to turn to Henry Walford Davies (1869-1941). Vaughan Williams and Walford Davies were rivals, and Vaughan Williams was prepared to endure an arduous two years of diligent tune-trawling in order to make sure that Walford Davies got nowhere near the *English Hymnal*.

Of the seven early-20th century arrangers represented in this anthology, only two – Henry Balfour Gardiner (1877-1950) and Harold Darke (1888-1976) – were born in London rather than in the shires. More pertinently, all but one of them studied composition at the Royal College of Music under Stanford – only Balfour Gardiner, who studied in Frankfurt, did not. Stanford's reputation as a teacher was that of an unmethodical, opinionated, outspoken autocrat, who detested slovenliness and vulgarity. Be that as it may, and in spite of his Irish upbringing and his period of study in Leipzig, Stanford nurtured an entire generation of composers whose musical outlook was technically sensitive and viscerally English. The only composer represented here by more arrangements than Vaughan Williams is another Stanford pupil, Gustav Holst (1874-1934). Apart from Darke and Balfour Gardiner, the other Stanford pupils whose music appears in this anthology are Rutland Boughton (1878-1960), Reginald Morris (1886-1948), and George Dyson (1883-1964).

Determining the provenance of folk songs is notoriously difficult. But, on the face of it, ten songs in this collection seem to have originated in Scotland. 'Ca' the yowes' is one of Vaughan Williams's most popular arrangements; its delicately resonant choral harmonies and plangent tenor solo have made it a fixture of secular recitals for many years. 'Ho-ro, my nut-brown maiden' is an example of a Gaelic work song, 'Dream Angus' of a Celtic lullaby, 'The Piper o' Dundee' a Jacobite rallying cry, and 'Màiri Bhàn's Wedding' is also known as the Lewis Bridal Song and hails from the Outer Hebrides. Four of the songs here have words by Scotland's national poet, Robert Burns (1756-96), the Bard of Ayrshire. Interestingly, 'My love is like a red, red rose' is related to the English song 'The Turtle Dove' and 'Ae fond kiss' to an Irish tune by the blind Irish harper Ruaidhrí Dáll Ó Catháin (Rory Dall). 'The De'il cam fiddlin' thro' the town' is an autobiographical parody. Excisemen were employees of the crown, who collected taxes and intercepted illegal goods – such people were deeply unpopular in the late 18th century. Yet Burns himself worked as an exciseman from 1789 until his death, and this humorous song celebrates the fact that the exciseman has been taken to hell by the Devil. By contrast, 'Auld Lang Syne' is a nostalgic song that is used to usher in the New Year or to bid farewell to the deceased at funerals. Burns also collected the 17th-century ballad 'The Raggle Taggle Gipsies', which tells the story of opportunistic John Faa, leader of a band of outlaws, and Lady Jane Hamilton, who was unhappily married to the Earl of Cassilis: lovable rogue beds classy lady – a fabulously well-worn stereotype.

Three arrangements of Welsh tunes grace this collection: the love song 'Tra bo dau'; 'My sweetheart's like Venus' (the ninth in Holst's 1931 collection of *Twelve Welsh Folk Songs*); and 'All through the night', whose tune 'Ar Hyd y Nos' appeared in the Evening section of the *English Hymnal* married to posthumously published words by the second Bishop of Calcutta, Reginald Heber, 'God that madest earth and heaven'. There are also three arrangements of Northumbrian tunes, two of which were originally pipe-tunes: the octave leaps of 'Bonny at morn' testify to the instrumental genesis of the melody and 'Blow the wind southerly' is one of Tyneside's better-known exports with words by John Stobbs. 'Dance to your daddy' would appear to be as Geordie as brown ale, yet 'daddie' could well be the original Scottish term and 'minnie' (as used in other versions of the song) the later Newcastle variant.

Somerset is England's best represented county in this collection with four songs. R.O. Morris's arrangement of 'High Germany' is a melancholy farewell and 'The Ship in Distress' is an adventure ballad. 'Dashing Away with the Smoothing Iron' is transmitted as 'Driving Away...' in some sources and its tune bears more than passing resemblance to 'All around my hat', Steeleye Span's only other 1970s hit single apart from 'Gaudete'. 'O Waly Waly' was published by Cecil Sharp in his 1906 collection *Songs from Somerset*, although the song is more likely to be of Scottish origin. This beautiful artefact represents a family of texts rather than a single song, and its development shows the transition from ballad to lyric.

The southern English counties of Sussex and Cornwall are each represented by two songs. John Broadwood collected 'The Bailiff's Daughter of Islington' in Sussex in 1843 and 'The Devil and the Ploughman' is also known as the 'Sussex Whistling Song'. The athletic 'Going up Camborne Hill' is clearly placed in Cornwall by its title, although 'I love my love' is more obviously set in Moorfields in the City of London rather than the West Country. Holst's setting of 'I love my love' is immensely sophisticated and takes the listener away from the plagal modes of Cornish folk song and into harmonic territory that is altogether more impressionistic.

The rest of England is covered from bottom to top by 'The [onomatopoeic] Song of the Blacksmith' (a cobbler in some versions) from Hampshire, 'Bushes and Briars' from Essex, 'Yarmouth Town' from Suffolk, 'Come lasses and lads' from Lincolnshire, and the riddle ballad 'Scarborough Fair' from Yorkshire. 'Come lasses and lads' is also known as 'The Rural Dance around the Maypole' and is a versification of Scene II of Thomas Heywood's play *A Woman Killed with Kindness* of 1607, while 'Scarborough Fair' was collected from a Whitby fisherman in 1891, where it also known as 'Whittingham Fair'; the tune also turns up in parts of Scandinavia.

Culturally, the most exotic items of this volume are to be found in the Manx song 'Mannin Veen' ('Dear Isle of Man') and the 18th-century sea shanty 'The Rio Grande', which was sung by Merseyside sailors as they set out on their journey to liberate newly discovered gold in Brazil's Rio Grande do Sul. Additionally there is a 17th-century work (the Beggars' Chorus, which a century later, in the hands of Thomas Arne, became 'A-hunting we will go'), a 16th-century piece ('The Three Ravens', which was later published by Thomas Ravenscroft in his collection *Melismata* of 1611), and Holst's composition based on the words of a 15th-century wassail, 'Bring us in good ale'. Today we might understand wassailing to mean the act of going from house to house at Christmas singing carols. But originally the word wassail came from the Old Norse *vesheill*, via the Middle English *wæshæil*, eventually to emerge as *washeil* ('be in good health'), with its response *drincheil* ('drink good health'). The point is that wassailing shouldn't just be for Christmas and New Year; you may toast people all year round. And folk song shouldn't be restricted to the village green any more than classical music should be restricted to the concert hall. This collection exists to encourage choral singers to discover their inner folklore. The worst that can happen is that you will engage with some haunting tunes and some perplexing storylines. The best is that you might open your mind to a whole new world of musico-poetic expression.

Jeremy Summerly
Royal Academy of Music, London, 2015

Acknowledgements

Designing a collection such as this is no small task, and thanks is due to a large number of people who have helped in the long process of collating and editing the material, in particular to Meirion Wynn Jones for his guidance and transliterations of the Welsh texts, Bob Carswell for his transliterations of the Manx text, Michael Emery and all at the BBC Singers archive for their immensely helpful support and time; Jonathan Wikeley, Chris Ballam, Tom Farncombe, Matthew Berry, Ruth Keating, and Paul and Julie Ewers at Novello; and Amy Bebbington, Jeremy Summerly, Christopher Bell, Andrew Millinger and all at the Herbert Howells Trust.

THE NOVELLO BOOK *of*

BRITISH FOLKSONGS

Ae fond kiss

Scottish folksong
Robert Burns (1759-96)

arr. Paul Mealor (b. 1975)

4

A-hunting We Will Go

'The Beggars' Chorus'
Thomas Arne (1710-78)
Henry Fielding (1707-54)

arr. John Creed (1904-74)

Tempo I

home-ward hun-gry we__ re-turn, To feast__ a-way__ the night,_____ to

home-ward hun-gry we re-turn, To feast__ a-way the night, to

home-ward hun-gry we re-turn, To feast__ a-way the night, to

home-ward hun-gry we re-turn, To feast__ a-way the night,_____ to

Tempo I

feast__ a-way the night. Then a-drink-ing we will

feast__ a-way the night. Then a-drink-ing we will

feast__ a-way the night. Then a-drink-ing we will go,_____ a-

feast__ a-way the night. Then a-drink-ing we will go,_____ a-

l.h.

mf

legg.

All Through the Night

Welsh folksong

arr. Grayston Ives (b. 1948)

'do' should be sung with a long 'oo'.

In order to support the melody, some tenors may wish to join the baritones in bars 13–16 and 30–33.

Souls from heav'n, their bless - ings bring - ing songs of love for

ev - er sing - ing Through the vale of dark - ness ring - ing

night,_____ On the earth, with light so ten- der,

all through the night,_____ But, when age brings

grief   and   sad - ness,   join   our   hearts   with   love   and glad - ness,

do   do do do do   do do do   do do do   do do   dm

With   the   light   of   heav'n   sur-round   us   all   through   the

Auld Lang Syne

Scottish folksong
Robert Burns (1759-96)

arr. Iain Farrington (b. 1977)

28

syne, my dear, for auld___ lang___ syne, We'll take a cup of

syne, my dear, for auld___ lang___ syne, We'll take a cup of

SOPRANO

kind - ness yet, for the sake of auld lang syne, for the sake of auld lang

ALTO

kind - ness yet, for the sake of auld, for the sake of auld lang syne, for the

TENOR & BASS

kind - ness yet, for the sake.___

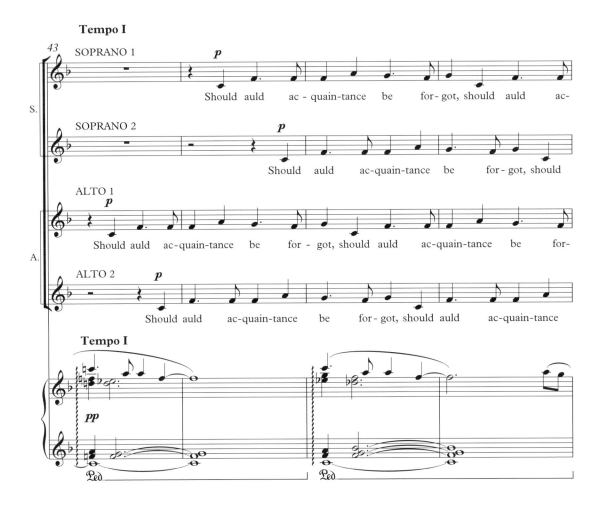

The Bailiff's Daughter of Islington

Sussex folksong

arr. Harold Darke (1888-1976)

fair Lon-don, an ap-pren-tice___ for to bind. And___ as she went a -

fair Lon-don, an ap-pren-tice___ for to bind.

fair Lon-don, an ap-pren-tice for to bind.

fair Lon - don,___ an ap-pren - tice___ for to bind.

-long the high___ road, the___ weath-er being hot and dry, She___

The weath-er being___ hot___ and___ dry,_____ She

The___ weath-er being___ hot___ and___ dry,_____ She___

The weath-er being dry,

stand - eth by thy side; She is here a - live, she

stand - eth by thy side; She is here a - live, she

She is here, she is here a - live, she

stand - eth by thy side; She is here a - live, she

is not dead, and rea - dy to be thy bride.

is not dead, and rea - dy to be thy bride.

is not dead, and rea - dy to be thy bride.

is not dead, and rea - dy to be thy bride.

31 March, 1917

Blow the wind southerly

Northumbrian folksong

arr. John Cameron (b. 1944)

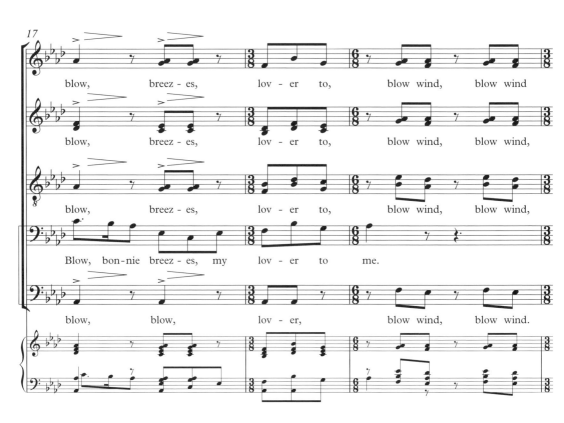

46

for the Palestine Choral Festival, August 2013

Bonny at Morn

Northumbrian folksong

arr. Jeremy Summerly (b. 1961)

neet = night   ower lang = over long

kye = cow

54

56

To Conrad Noel

Bring us in Good Ale

15th century

Gustav Holst (1874-1934)

onys = once, inought = enough

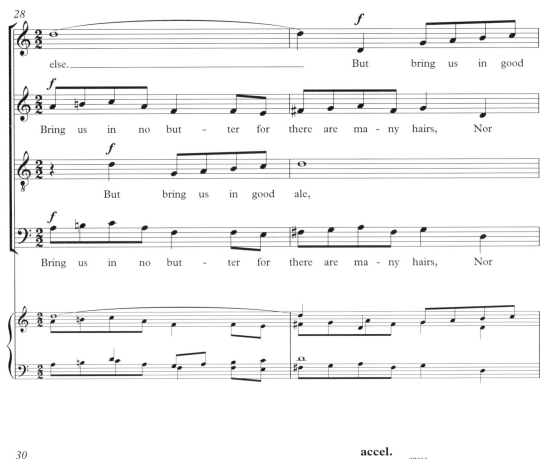

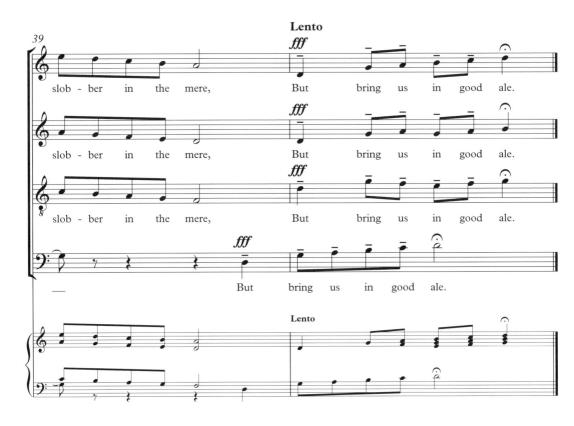

To The English Singers

Bushes and Briars

Essex Folksong

arr. Ralph Vaughan Williams
(1872-1958)

* Short 'u', as in the word 'but'

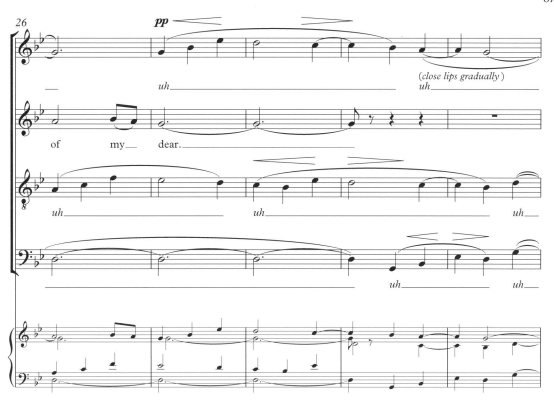

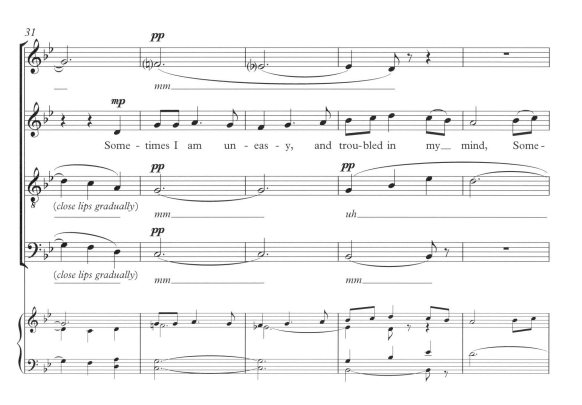

Ca' the yowes

Scottish folksong
Robert Burns (1759-96)

arr. Ralph Vaughan Williams
(1872-1958)

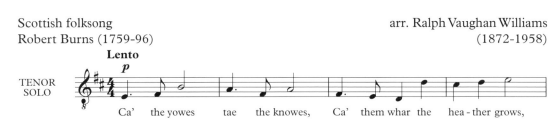

ca' the yowes tae the knowes = call the ewes to the knolls

Pronunciation: yowes = 'ow' always as in 'cow'.

burnie rows = river trickles

mavis' e'enin' = evening thrush

stown = stolen

★ With half-closed lips, a short 'u', as in the word 'but'.

a-fauldin' let us gang = let us get back to the fold

wimple = meander

lift = sky

blin' my e'e = blind my eye

TENOR SOLO

Pronunciation: in this instance, 'hie' and 'e'e' should rhyme with 'sea'.

Come lasses and lads

Lincolnshire folksong

arr. John Creed (1904-74)

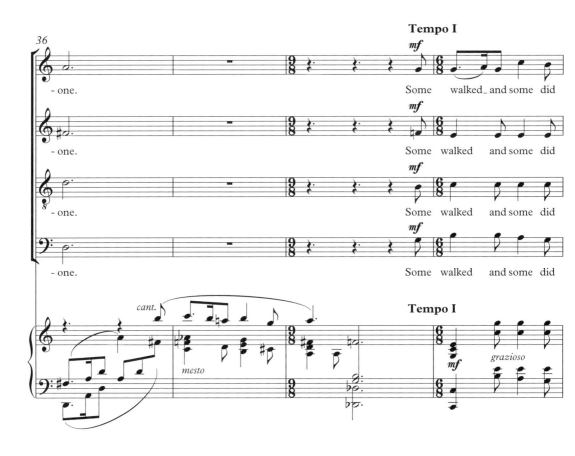

kis - ses twelve to meet___ next hol - i - day.___

kis - ses twelve to meet next hol - i - day.___

kis - ses twelve to meet next hol - i - day.___

kis - ses twelve to meet next hol - i - day.___

Poco meno mosso

Dance to your daddy

Northumbrian folksong

arr. David Stone (b. 1922)

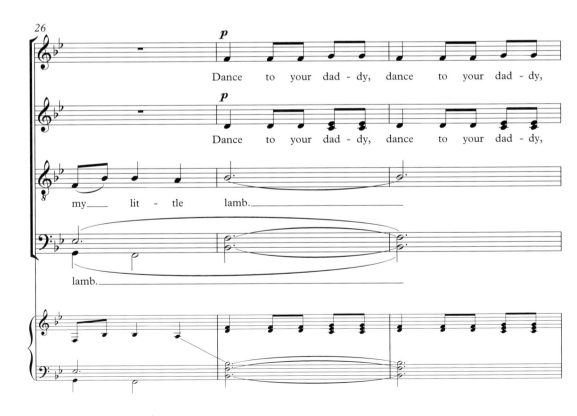

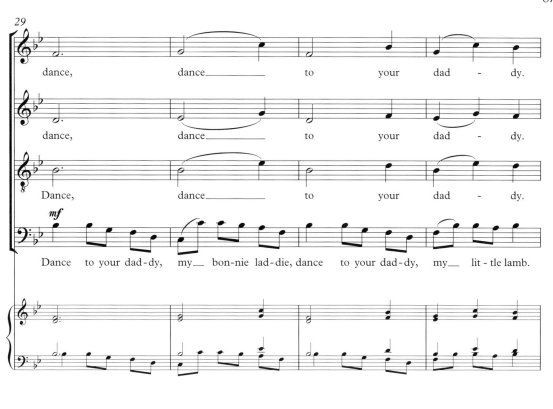

Dashing Away with the Smoothing Iron

Somerset folksong

arr. Keith Roberts (b. 1971)

for the Phoenix Singers of Shrewsbury

The De'il cam Fiddlin' thro' the Town

'The Hampdresser' (English Folksong)
Robert Burns (1759-96)

arr. Richard White (b. 1930)

Pronunciation: awa: as in 'awar'; maut (malt): as in 'mort'; town: 'toon'.

It is said that Burns found the tune, *The Hampdresser*, actually English, in *The Caledonian Pocket Companion* in which it had appeared having previously been published in *The Scots Musical Museum*.

ilka = every

mony braw = many good
meikle = big (not as big as 'mickle')

Pronunciation: foursome: as in 'hour'; strathspeys: 'strathspize'.

Pronunciation: ae (one, the very best): as in 'hay' (run a 'y' into it: 'the yay best dance').

The Devil and the Ploughman

Sussex folksong
'The Sussex Whistling Song'

arr. Betty Roe (b. 1930)

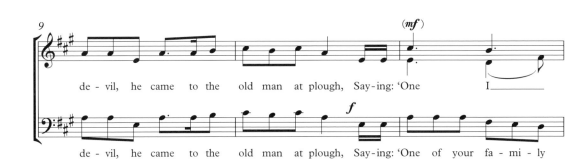

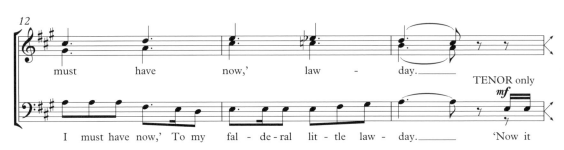

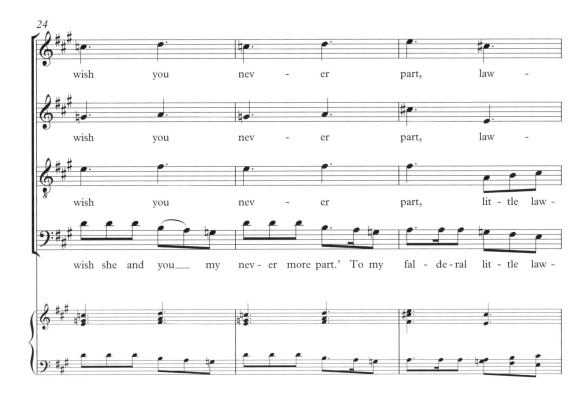

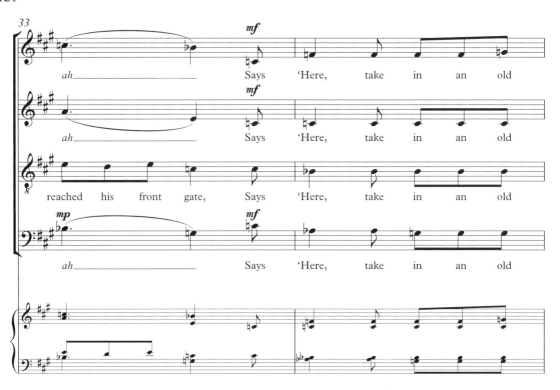

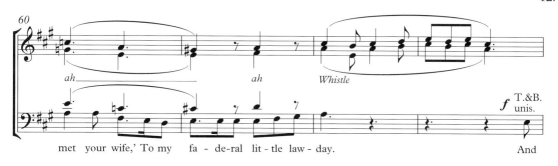

ah_____ ah Whistle

met your wife,' To my fa - de - ral lit - tle law - day. And

You see that the wo - men is

now to con - clude and make___ an end, the wo - men is

worse than the men, If they get sent to hell, they get kicked back a - gain, To my

worse than the men, Get sent to hell, kicked back a - gain,

accel.

molto cresc.

fal - de - ral lit - tle law, fal - de - ral lit - tle law,

molto cresc.

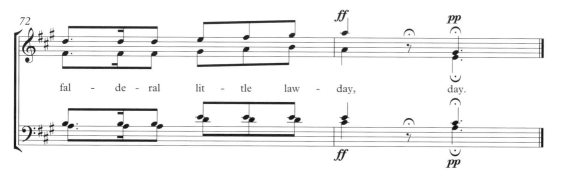

fal - de - ral lit - tle law - day, day.

Dream Angus

Scottish folksong

arr. Sheena Phillips (b. 1958)

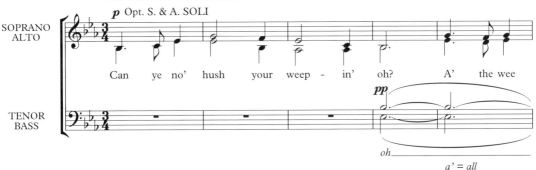

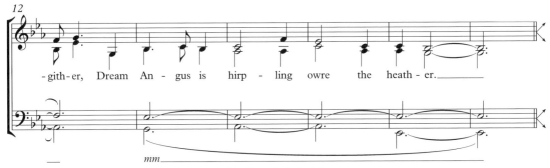

Pronunciation: a': English 'ah'; bairn: rhymes with 'cairn' (with frontal rolled 'r'); owre: 'hour';
thegither: the gither (hard 'g', hard 'th') to rhyme with 'the zither'

Angus is an ancient Celtic deity, associated in many stories with youth, beauty and love – though in others he is portrayed as a frightening figure or trickster, with power over death and the underworld. In this song he appears in his more benign guise as a bringer of sweet dreams.

fear,___ Dream An - gus has brought you a dream, my dear._____

mm_____

mm_____

-by, An - gus is here, my dear._____

SOPRANO 1 & 2
pp stagger breathing

S.

oo_____

ALTO
mp cantando

A. List to the cur - lew cry - in' oh, Faint - er the ech - oes

pp
stagger breathing

T.

oo_____

pp
stagger breathing

B.

oo_____

list = listen

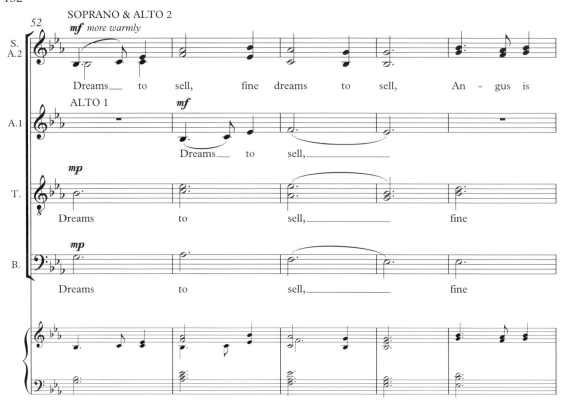

for Julia Carter

Going up Camborne Hill

Cornish folksong

Russell Pascoe (b. 1960)

Pronunciation: going = goin'; Camborne = Camburn; horses = 'osses

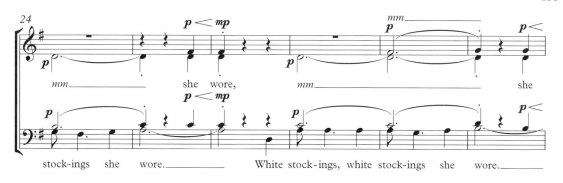

The hor-ses stood still, the wheels went a-round; Going

down.

up Cam-borne Hill, com-ing_ down, com-ing down.__

com-ing down.

S.

pa pa   pa pa   pa pa pa pa pa pa pa pa   pa pa   pa pa

A.

pa pa   pa pa   pa pa pa pa pa pa pa pa   pa pa   pa pa

T.

knowed her old fath-er, old man,_____ I knowed her old fath-er, old

B.

oom   oom   oom   oom pa pa oom   oom

(for rehearsal only)

Pronunciation: knowed, as in 'gnawed'; father, as in 'gather' (or 'feather' depending on the part of Cornwall.)

138

Pronunciation: heaved = haved (as in 'paved')

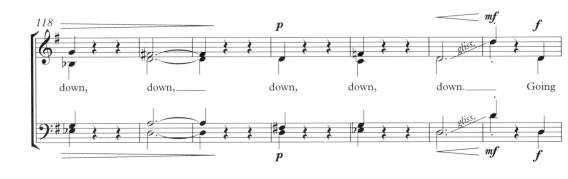

up Cam-borne Hill, com-ing____ down. Going up Cam-borne

com - ing down.

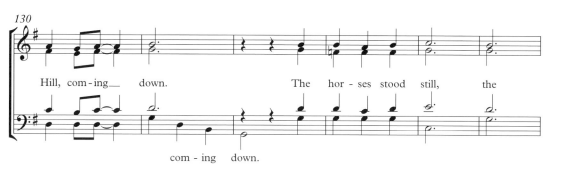

Hill, com-ing____ down. The hor - ses stood still, the

com - ing down.

accel. al fine

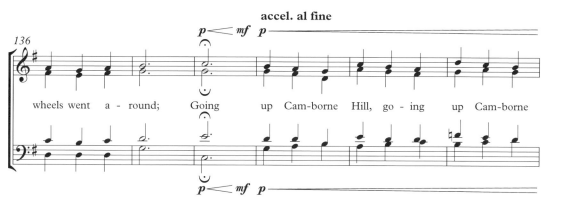

wheels went a - round; Going up Cam-borne Hill, go - ing up Cam-borne

Hill, go - ing up Cam-borne Hill, com-ing____ down.____

com - ing down.

High Germany

Somerset folksong

arr. Reginald (R.O.) Morris
(1888-1946)

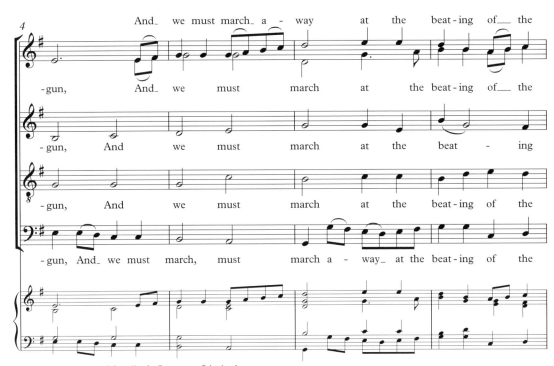

To the Glasgow Orpheus Choir

Ho-ro! my nut-brown maiden

Scottish folksong
Trans. J.S. Blackie (1809-95)

arr. George Dyson (1883-1964)

To C.K.S. and the Oriana

I Love my Love

Cornish folksong

arr. Gustav Holst (1874-1934)

Andante

SOPRANO

1. A - broad as I was walk-ing, one eve-ning in the spring, I

ALTO

1. A - broad as I was walk - ing, one eve - ning in the spring, I

TENOR

1. A - broad as I was walk - ing, one eve - ning in the spring, I

BASS

1. A - broad as I was walk - ing, one eve - ning in the spring, I

PIANO
(*for rehearsal only*)

Andante

heard a maid in Bed-lam so sweet-ly for to sing; Her chains she rat-tled

heard a maid in Bed - lam so sweet - ly for to sing; Her chains she rat-tled

heard a maid in Bed - lam so sweet - ly for to sing; Her chains she rat-tled

heard a maid in Bed - lam so sweet - ly for to sing; Her chains she rat-tled

with her hands, and thus re-pli-ed she: 'I love my love be-cause I know my

with her hands, and thus re-pli-ed she: mm___

with her hands, and thus re-pli-ed she:___ mm___

with her hands, and thus re-pli-ed she: mm___

love loves me! 2. O cru-el___ were___ his par-ents who___ sent my love to sea, And

mm___ 2. 'O cru-el were his par-ents who sent my love to sea, And

mm___ 2. 'O cru-el were___ his par-ents who sent my love to sea, And

mm___ 2. 'O cru-el were his par-ents who sent my love to sea, And___

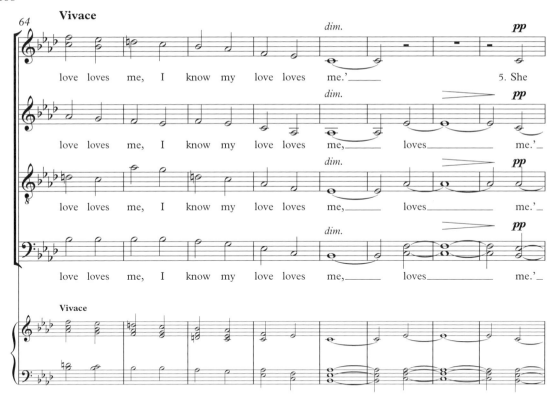

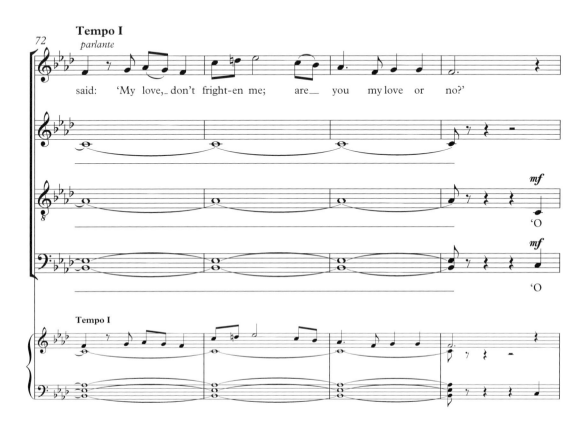

Màiri Bhàn's Wedding

Based on a Gaelic song
by John Bannerman (1865-1938)
Trans. Peter Hill and Sheena Phillips

arr. Sheena Phillips (b.1958)

Mài - ri Bhàn* makes my heart sing, Mài - ri Bhàn will wear my ring,

* Màiri Bhàn (fair Mary): pronounced 'mahree vahn'

She's my queen and I'm her king And we're going to mar - ry.

Mài - ri Bhàn makes my heart sing, Mài - ri Bhàn will wear my ring,

Mài - ri, Mài - ri Bhàn,

The expression 'Màiri Bhàn' is a familiar form of addressing a young woman.

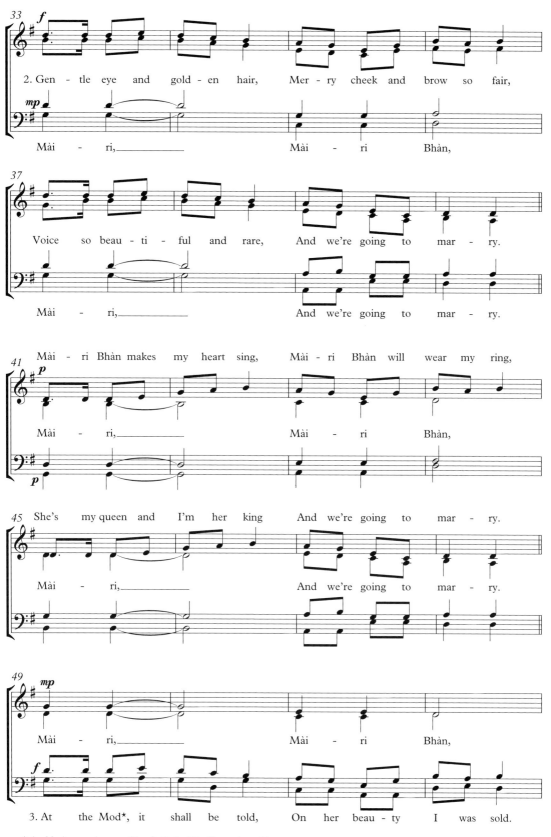

* the Mod: annual competitive festival of Gaelic music and language.

Mannin Veen

Manx folksong
from Dr Clague's MS Collection
Transliteration: Bob Carslake

arr. Ralph Vaughan Williams
(1872-1958)

* With half-closed lips, a short 'u', as in the word 'but'.

Pronunciation: the above text is a transliteration of the original Manx. tow = 'ow' as in 'cow'; lahul = with a long 'oo'; vay = 'ay' as in 'may'; logh = 'gh' as in Scottish 'loch'.

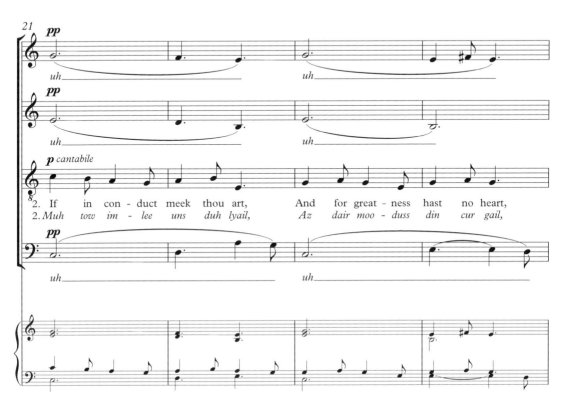

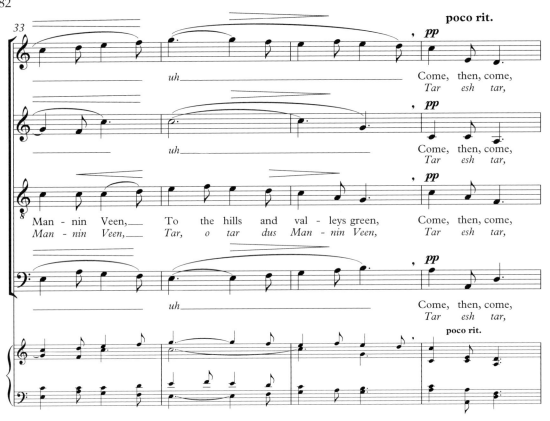

Poco meno mosso

Pronunciation: ghoo = 'gh' with a barely audible 'g'.

My love is like a red, red rose

Scottish folksong
Robert Burns (1759-1796)

arr. John Cameron (b. 1944)

190

My sweetheart's like Venus

Melody and Welsh words by
permission of Dr J. Lloyd Williams
Trans. Steuart Wilson
Transliteration: Meirion Wynn Jones

arr. Gustav Holst (1874-1934)

This needs an easy rhythm, not staccato, otherwise it is too jerky for the sentiment.
There are no indications of tempo or expression. These will arise out of the singing of the song,
and are left to the judgment of the conductor and the singers. G.H.

Pronunciation: In the transliteration, 'do' should be sung with a long 'oo'; bold ' **th** ' is voiced, as in 'the';
non-bold 'th' is unvoiced, as in 'thin'; bold ' **ch** ' as in 'loch'; 'ei' as in 'hay'.

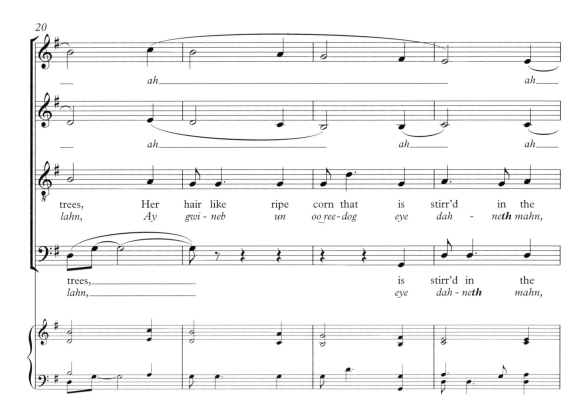

O Waly Waly

Somerset folksong

arr. Robert Rice (b. 1971)

'do' should be sung with a long 'oo'.

The Piper o' Dundee

Scottish folksong

arr. Ken Johnston (b. 1962)

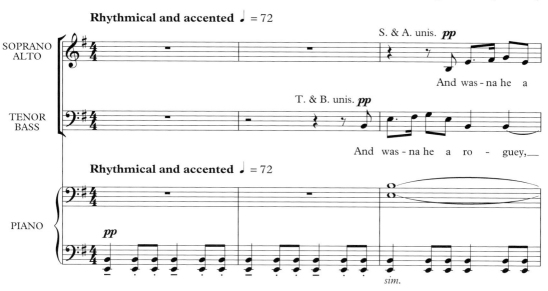

The melody was published in Neil Stewart's collection of 1761. The lyrics were published in James Hogg's *Jacobite Relics* Vol. 2 of 1821. The song names several pro-Jacobite pipe tunes and songs.

pip - er o' Dun - dee._____ The pip - er cam tae oor toon, tae

-dee._____

oor_ toon, tae oor_ toon, the pip - er cam tae oor toon, and he played bon - nie - lie._____

bonnielie = beautifully

He played a spring the laird to please, a spring brent-new frae 'yont the seas, and

brent-new = brand new
'yont = beyond

bags = bagpipes

27

'Ye'se be fou and I'se be fain', and 'Auld Stu-art's back a-gain', wi' mu-ckle mirth and glee.

and 'Auld Stu-art's back a-gain', wi' mu-ckle mirth and glee.

muckle = much

30

He played 'The Kirk', he played 'The Queer', 'The Mul-lin Dhu', and 'Che-va-lier', and

He played 'The Kirk', he played 'The Queer', 'The Mul-lin Dhu', and 'Che-va-lier', and

33

A little faster ♩ = 88

'Lang a-wa but wel-come here', sae sweet, sae bon-nie-lie.

unis. *mf*

'Lang a-wa but wel-come here', sae sweet, sae bon-nie-lie. And

A little faster ♩ = 88

mf

nane = none

mad their lane = on their own

mo-ny a vow o' weir was ta'en that nicht at A-mul-rie. There was

mo-ny a vow o' weir was ta'en that nicht at A-mul-rie. There was

sim.

mony = many   *weir = war*

Tul-li-bard-ine and Bur-leigh, and Stru-an, Keith and Og-il-vie, and

Tul-li-bard-ine and Bur-leigh, and Stru-an, Keith and Og-il-vie, and

brave Car-ne-gie, wha but he, the pip-er o' Dun-dee.

brave Car-ne-gie, wha but he, the pip-er o' Dun-dee. And

wha = who

The Raggle Taggle Gipsies

Scottish folksong

arr. Rutland Boughton (1878-1960)

sang so low, The la - dy sat in her cham - ber late, Her

sang so low, The la - dy___ sat in her cham - ber late, Her

sang so low, The la - dy___ sat in her cham - ber___ late, Her

sang so low, The la - dy sat in her cham - ber late, Her

heart it melt - ed a - way like snow. They___ sang so sweet, they___

heart it melt - ed a - way___ like snow. They___ sang so sweet,___ they___

heart it melt - ed a - way___ like___ snow. They sang___ so___ sweet, they___

heart it melt - ed a - way like snow. They sang so sweet,___ they___

in loving memory of Pam Ehrlich

The Rio Grande

18th-century sea shanty

arr. Stephen Jackson (b. 1951)

Written for the Last Night of the Proms 2004 when, with some consternation, it was performed simultaneously by the Hallé Choir conducted by John Wilson in Manchester Cathedral Gardens, and the BBC Symphony Orchestra conducted by Leonard Slatkin in the Royal Albert Hall, London.

Way_____ for Ri - o!_____ We'll heave up the an-chor to this jol - ly sound, And we're

We'll heave up the an-chor to

Way_____ for Ri - o!_____ We'll heave the an-chor to this jol - ly sound, And we're

poco tenuto   **a tempo**

bound for the Ri - o Grande!

bound for the Ri - o Grande!

poco tenuto   **a tempo**

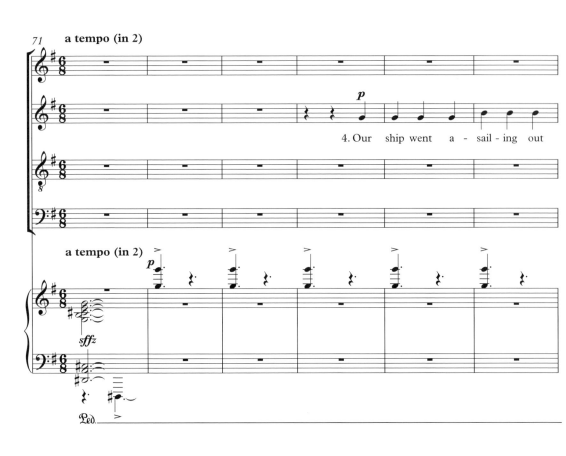

Scarborough Fair

Yorkshire folksong

arr. Iain Farrington (b. 1977)

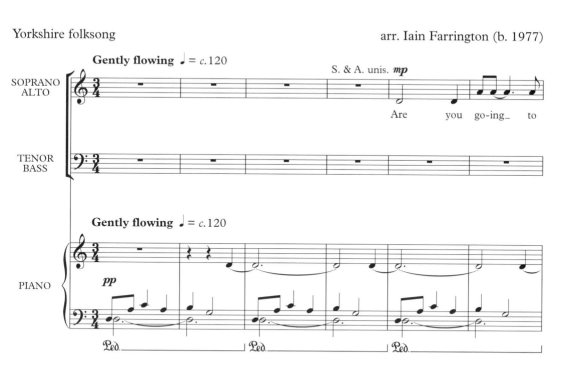

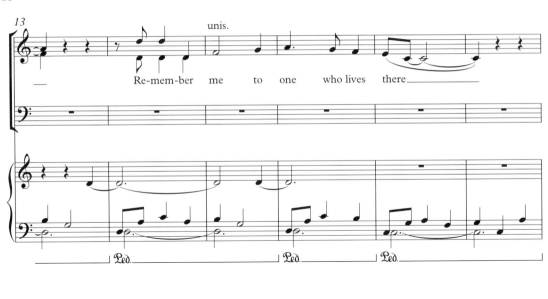

Re-mem-ber me to one who lives there_____

For once_ he_ was_____ a true love of_ mine._____

p T. & B. unis.

mm_____

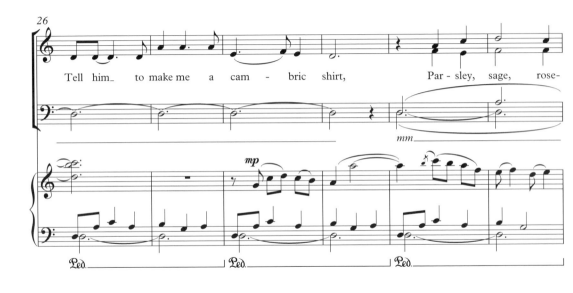

Tell him_ to make me a cam - bric shirt, Par - sley, sage, rose-

mm_____

mp

for Tim

The Ship in Distress

Sussex folksong

arr. Geoffrey White (b. 1944)

This English folksong was collected by George Butterworth from the singing of Mr Harwood of Watersfield, Sussex, in 1907. The second verse describes the dire adversity suffered by the seamen and the second choir quotes Herbert Howells's Psalm Prelude Set 1, no. 1 (Op. 32) which is inscribed 'Lo, the poor crieth, and the Lord heareth him, yea and saveth him out of all his trouble' (Psalm 34, v. 6).

* If preferred, this passage may be sung in unison (Choir 1) with piano accompaniment.
  If both choirs sing, the passage should be sung unaccompanied.

fel - lows, they stood in a tot - ter, a - cast - ing lots as to which should die, The

mm_____ mm_____ mm_____

mm_____ mm_____

mm_____ mm_____

mm_____ mm_____

mm_____ mm_____

CHOIR 1 S. & A.

lot it fell on Ro-bert Jack-son, Whose fa - mi - ly was so ve - ry great. 'I'm

FULL VOICES

free to die, but oh! my com-rades, let me keep look out till the break of day.' 3. A

to C.K.S. and the Oriana

The Song of the Blacksmith

Hampshire folksong
collected by G.B. Gardiner

arr. Gustav Holst (1874-1934)

first he won_ my heart, till he wrote to me a let-ter. With his

kang kang ki ki kang kang kang kang

kang kang ki ki kang kang kang kang

kang kang ki ki kang kang kang kang

ham-mer in_ his_ hand, as he strikes so_ might-y and clev-er

kang kang kang kang

With his ham-mer in_ his_ hand, as he strikes so_ might-y and

kang kang kang kang

264

There were three ravens

from Thomas Ravenscroft
Melismata (1611)

arr. Henry Balfour Gardiner
(1877-1950)

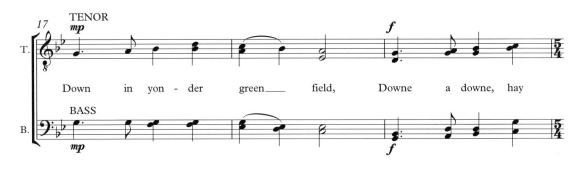

Down in yon-der green___ field, Downe a downe, hay

downe hay downe, There lies a knight slain un-der his shield, With a

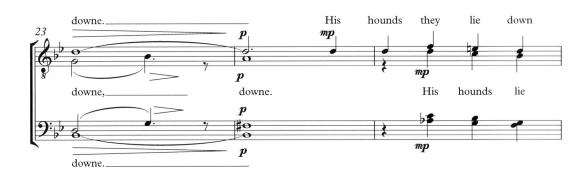

downe.___ His hounds they lie down

downe,___ downe. His hounds lie

downe.___

at his feet, So well___ they can their mas - ter

Tra bo dau

Welsh folksong
Translation and transliteration:
Meirion Wynn Jones

arr. Meirion Wynn Jones (b. 1972)

The one my heart loves lives far from here,

And in my longing to see her, my complexion fades.

Pronunciation: In the transliteration, 'do' should be sung with a long 'oo'; bold ' **th** ' is voiced, as in 'the';
non-bold 'th' is unvoiced, as in 'thin'; bold ' **ch** ' as in 'loch'; 'ei' as in 'hay'.

A thousand times fairer is she than the dawn's hue,

And her love is to me a treasure greater
than the riches of this world.

mun, Na chy - foeth byd____ a'i fri. Cy-foeth nid yw ond o - fer - edd,____
mean, Na chuh - voyth bead____ eye vree. Cuh-voyth nid eew ond o - ver - eth,____

mun, Na chy - foeth byd____ a'i fri. Cy-foeth nid yw ond o - fer - edd,____
mean, Na chuh - voyth bead____ eye vree. Cuh-voyth nid eew ond o - ver - eth,____

mun, Na chy - foeth byd____ a'i fri.____ Cy-foeth nid yw ond o - fer - edd,____
mean, Na chuh - voyth bead____ eye vree.____ Cuh-voyth nid eew ond o - ver - eth,____

mun, Na chy - foeth byd a'i fri. Cy-foeth nid yw ond o - fer - edd,____
mean, Na chu - voyth bead eye vree. Cuh-voyth nid eew ond o - ver - eth,____

Riches are but vanity,

Glen-did nid yw yn par-hau, Ond ca-riad pur sydd fel y____ dur Yn pa - ra
Glen-deed nid eew un par-high, Ond ca-riad peer sith vel uh____ deer Un pa - ra

Glen-did nid yw yn par - hau,____ Ond ca-riad pur sydd fel y dur Yn pa - ra
Glen-deed nid eew un par - high,____ Ond ca-riad peer sith vel uh deer Un pa - ra

Glen-did nid yw yn par - hau,____ Ond ca-riad pur sydd fel y dur____ Yn pa - ra
Glen-deed nid eew un par - high,____ Ond ca-riad peer sith vel uh deer____ Un pa - ra

Glen-did nid yw yn par-hau, Ond ca-riad pur sydd fel y dur Yn pa - ra
Glen-deed nid eew un par-high, Ond ca-riad peer sith vel uh deer Un pa - ra

Beauty will fade away,   *But true love, as strong as steel,*

Will endure while there are two.

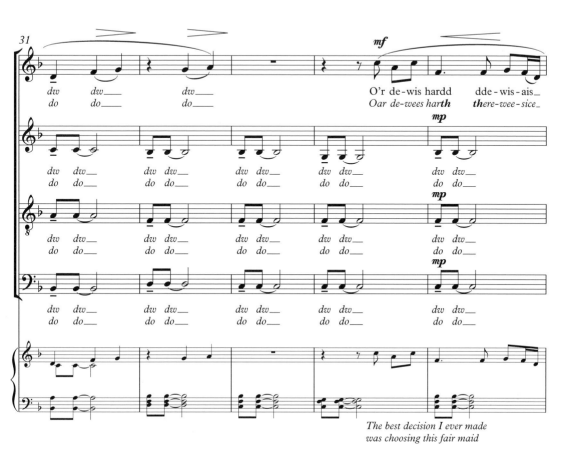

The best decision I ever made
was choosing this fair maid

282

And fire will freeze over before I regret it.

Though I suffer love's sickness,
I hope that she is well -

From the depths of my heart
I adore the ground on which she treads.

The collecting of **'Tra bo dau'** in 1906 by the Bangor academic, J. Lloyd Williams (1854-1945) from the singing of his wife and sister-in-law, proved to be an act of great consequence for the future of folk music in Wales - leading as it did, to the founding of the Welsh Folk Song Society. The song, promoted by Williams at the National Eisteddfod in Caernarfon that year, grew quickly in popularity, despite the commentator, Frank Kidson claiming the melody to be, "a corruption of, 'The Cobler of Castlebury'" [*sic*] by Charles Dibdin (1745-1814). More recent analysis points to a similarity in the song's opening phrase only. MWJ

Yarmouth Town

Suffolk folksong

arr. Ian Assersohn

won't you come down, won't you come down, won't you come down to Yar-mouth Town?

Won't you come down, won't you come down, won't you come down to Yar-mouth Town? *Hey!*

8. Come

dm   dm   dm   dm   dm   dm   dm   dm

FRENCH SONGS & CHORUSES

for mixed-voice choir

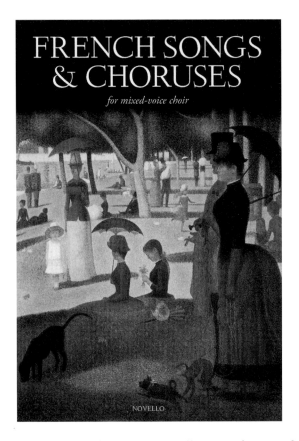

French songs and choruses for choirs is a collection of some of the finest original choral music by French composers, and delightful arrangements of some of the greatest and most beautiful French songs. The volume is suitable for choirs of all sizes and abilities, and makes for a fine concert programme in itself, as well as being an inviting treasure trove of pieces to dip into.

Order No.: NOV165198